THE GRAND CANYON NATIONAL PARK COLORING BOOK

Illustrations by Gary A. Bloomfield

Text by Helen Henkel Larson

An Earthwalk Press Publication

Grand Canyon National Park

Hello! Welcome to Grand Canyon National Park! Established in 1919, the park preserves one of the world's deepes[t] canyons. The powerful Colorado River has carved a canyon that is nearly a mile deep and 277 river miles long into th[e] Kaibab Plateau. At Mather Point on the South Rim, many visitors obtain their first glimpse into the breathtaking Gran[d] Canyon. The point is named for Steven Mather, the National Park Service's first director.

Pictographs   Split-twig Figurine   Anasazi Pottery   Navajo Weaving   Hopi Kachina
Hopi Silver Necklace (Modern)   Turquoise Stones

Native American Cultures

eople have lived at Grand Canyon for over 4000 years. About 2500 BC, the earliest inhabitants left small split-twig
gurines in caves. The Anasazi lived here for about 500 years, leaving around 1150 AD. They built permanent dwellings,
ade pottery and farmed. Later the Havasupai, whose descendants still live in the western canyon, left pictographs—
ck paintings. Today, the Hopi and Navajo tribes live east of the canyon. Both have rich spiritual and artistic cultures.

Steller's Jay

Camping is a good way to learn more about the park and its inhabitants. The Steller's jay is a frequent—and noisy—campground visitor. This deep blue bird is the only crested jay west of the Rocky Mountains. Its loud, harsh call is heard throughout the forest. The Steller's jay can mimic the scream of a hawk. Please remember all park animals are wild, and do not feed them. You are a visitor in their home.

Exploring the Colorado River Canyons

Major John Wesley Powell scientifically explored much of the unknown Southwest, naming many of its features. He and is eight-man crew were the first explorers to run the Colorado River through the Grand Canyon. In 1869, their journey ook three months and six days from Green River, Wyoming, to Grand Wash Cliffs, Arizona. The men braved dangerous apids in four small boats, with the one-armed Powell perched on a chair lashed to the deck.

Hiking Through Space and Time

A hike into the Grand Canyon is a hike through both space and time. When you descend from the North Rim, it is as you began walking in Canada. For every 1000 vertical feet you drop, the change is equal to moving 300 miles southwar across flat country! Your hike crosses communities ranging from British Columbia's moist evergreen forests to Mexico arid Sonoran desert. And you journey among rock walls that record nearly 2 billion ears of Earth's history!

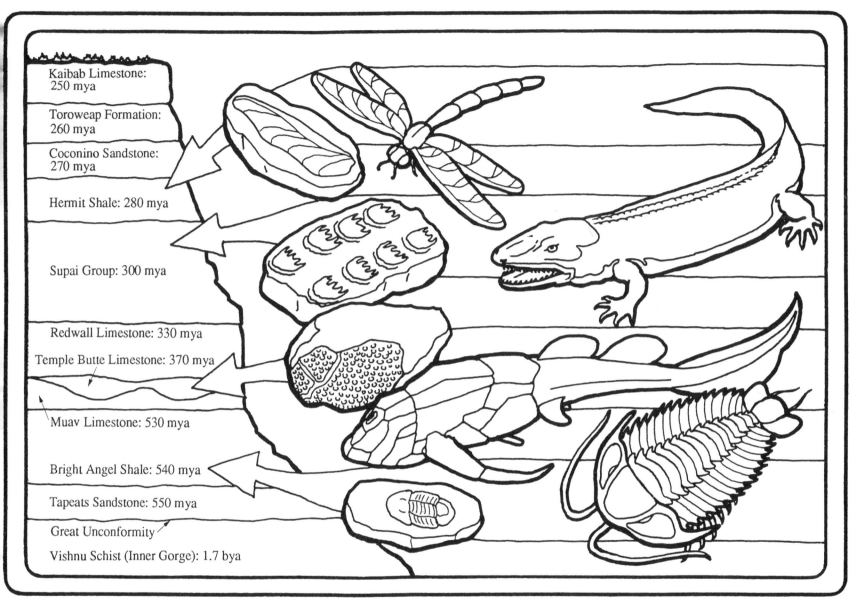

Kaibab Limestone: 250 mya

Toroweap Formation: 260 mya

Coconino Sandstone: 270 mya

Hermit Shale: 280 mya

Supai Group: 300 mya

Redwall Limestone: 330 mya

Temple Butte Limestone: 370 mya

Muav Limestone: 530 mya

Bright Angel Shale: 540 mya

Tapeats Sandstone: 550 mya

Great Unconformity

Vishnu Schist (Inner Gorge): 1.7 bya

Geological cross-section represents sedimentary layers above Great Unconformity   mya=million years ago   bya=billion years ago

Nearly Two Billion Years of Earth's History

The Grand Canyon records almost half of Earth's 4.6 billion year history. The Vishnu Schist that forms the Inner Gorge is some of Earth's oldest exposed rock: 1.7 billion years old. Fossils help scientists determine what environments were like. For example, a dragonfly's wing (Hermit Shale) and amphibian tracks (Supai Formation) suggest swamps or lagoons. A plate from a primitive "armored" fish (Temple Butte Limestone) and a trilobite (Bright Angel Shale) indicate seas.

Red Squirrel   Clark's Nutcracker   Wild Turkey

White Cranesbill

The Spruce–Fir–Aspen Forest

The Grand Canyon contains a great variety of life. Climate and elevation change radically between the canyon bottom (2400 feet) and the North Rim (8800 feet). Plants and animals change, as well, reacting to differences in temperature, available water, elevation and soil. The North Rim receives about twice as much rainfall as the South Rim does, and the winter snows are deeper and longer lasting. The increased moisture and richer, deeper soil support the Engelman

Skyrocket   Mule Deer   Broad-tailed Hummingbird   Western Yarrow   Quaking Aspen

The Spruce–Fir–Aspen Forest

pruce–subalpine fir–quaking aspen forest above 8500 feet. Lush wildflower meadows provide perfect habitat for urrowing animals like moles. Mule deer browse in forest clearings. Wild turkey gobblers (males) strut for their hens. A nale broad-tailed hummingbird is a swift splash of ruby and emerald as he sips nectar from the skyrocket's red, trumpet-haped flowers. A red squirrel noisily defends his territory, while a Clark's nutcracker searches for cones to "crack."

Mule Deer   Striped Skunk   Gambel Oak   Abert Squirrel
                                                   Mountain Chickadee

The Ponderosa Pine Forest

The ponderosa pine grows below the spruce–fir–aspen forest on the North Rim and away from the edge on the South
Rim where more moisture and soil are available. The ponderosa is adapted to drier conditions than most pines. This
handsome tree has reddish bark that forms scaly plates. The Gambel oak intermingles with the ponderosa; its acorns
are in important food for wildlife. Many birds make this forest their home. The mountain chickadee—a black-capped

Elderberry   Steller's Jay   Bobcat   Ponderosa Pine   White-breasted Nuthatch
                                    Purple Cranesbill

The Ponderosa Pine Forest

lack-bibbed acrobat—checks an elderberry for insects under the watchful eye of a Steller's jay. A white-breasted nut-
atch descends a trunk headfirst in search of insects or larva. A tassel-eared Abert squirrel scampers along a limb, its
ong tail flowing behind. This squirrel is largely dependent on the ponderosa pine for food. Towards evening, long-eared
nule deer are often seen. Night hunters, like the striped skunk and secretive bobcat, prowl the forest.

Pinyon Pine   Raven   Claretcup Cactus   Turkey Vulture   Pinyon Jay

Cliff Chipmunk   Cliffrose

The Pinyon–Juniper Woodland

The pinyon–juniper woodland is the South Rim's main community. Plants here must be good moisture conserver because the South Rim only receives about 15 inches of rain a year. The pinyon pine and Utah juniper possess smal waxy leaves that reduce water loss and have insulating bark that retains moisture. Cliffrose, claret cup cactus and banan yucca are also adapted to these dry conditions. The scrubby, twisted junipers and pinyons provide food, homes and cove

Banana Yucca   Gray Flycatcher   Utah Juniper   Scrub Jay   Desert Cottontail

The Pinyon—Juniper Woodland

or wildlife. Pinyon jays, which are fond of pinyon nuts, nest and feed here. From its juniper perch, a gray flycatcher repares to dart after a flying insect. Cliff chipmunks scamper along the rim, storing nuts and seeds for winter. A desert ottontail, startled by a noisy scrub jay, hides beneath a juniper. Riding the canyon updrafts, a turkey vulture spies the emains of an unlucky cottontail. The raven—a great opportunist—watches the community's activities with interest.

Rock Wren   Desert Bighorn   Utah Agave   Banana Yucca

Collared Lizard   Red-tailed Hawk

The Tonto Plateau

Life on the Tonto Plateau, 3000 feet below the South Rim, is adapted to high desert conditions. Vegetation is sparse and root systems have evolved to quickly gather the infrequent water. The grey-green blackbrush is the most commo plant, often forming nearly pure stands. Utah agave, banana yucca and various cacti grow here also. The white-taile antelope squirrel is well adapted to this arid habitat since it can obtain all its water from its food. The black-throate

Black-throated Sparrow
Blackbrush

Coyote   American Kestrel   White-tailed Antelope Squirrel

The Tonto Plateau

sparrow also tolerates heat and drought, trilling its high, sweet song. The rock wren—who is also a good singer—makes path of rock chips to its nest in a rock crevice. An aggressive male collared lizard defends his territory around a large ock. Hunters, like coyote, red-tailed hawk and American kestrel, watch for unwary antelope squirrels and other prey. he elusive bighorn sure-footedly travels the sheer canyon walls, leaping from rock to rock with great agility.

Mourning Dove

Barrel Cactus

Say's Phoebe

Prickly Pear

Grand Canyon Rattlesnake

Western Whiptail Lizard

The Canyon Floor

The canyon floor is the hottest, driest environment. Yearly precipitation averages 7 inches. Summer temperatures reach 110°F and are intensified by the black schist walls. Cacti and reptiles are well adapted to this desert habitat. Mesquit provides food, cover or nesting sites for Lucy's warblers, skunks, coyotes and others. Most animals lie low during th day's heat. Early morning finds the nocturnal spotted skunk returning to its burrow. Cold-blooded reptiles, like th

actus   Sacred Datura   White-throated Swift   Spotted Skunk   Mesquite   Lucy's Warbler
                          Brittlebush   Beavertail Cactus   Chuckwalla

The Canyon Floor

huckwalla, western collared lizard and Grand Canyon rattlesnake, warm themselves on sunny rocks. Cactus blossoms en, adding their colors to the brilliant yellow of brittlebush. In contrast, the white trumpets of night-blooming sacred atura will wilt as soon as the sun hits them. The soft cooing of a male mourning dove announces his courtship flight. A ay's phoebe darts out to catch a flying insect snack. Above the river, white-throated swifts soar, scooping up insects.

Yellow Columbine   Watercress   Tadpoles   Black-chinned Hummingbird   Crimson Monkeyflower   Canyon Wren
Canyon Tree Frog   Maidenhair Fern   Twining Snapdragon

A Desert Oasis

Springs create oases where moisture-loving plants and animals survive. Maidenhair fern cascades in shady nooks that ar[e] brightened in summer by blossoms of crimson monkeyflower and purple twining snapdragon. Frogs catch insects fro[m] mossy rocks; tadpoles—future frogs—swim in shallow pools amid watercress. The silence is broken by a canyon wren['s] song and the rapidly beating wings of a black-chinned hummingbird feeding on nectar from a yellow columbine.

Wildflowers

he purple cranesbill (left) is a common woodland flower in the ponderosa pine forest. Its long, beaked fruit resembles crane's bill. Claretcup hedgehog cactus (center) grows from the rims to the canyon floor. Its blossoms are a brilliant d with green stigmas in the center. The cliffrose (right) is an important member of the juniper–pinyon pine woodland. s profuse cream flowers are very fragrant. Cliffrose provides winter browse for deer.

Abert Squirrel

Kaibab Squirrel

Tassel-eared Squirrels

As the Colorado River carved the Grand Canyon, it slowly widened the gap between the two rims. The tassel-eared squirrels were unable to cross this barrier, so the squirrels isolated on each side developed different characteristics. The South Rim's Abert squirrel is grey with white underparts and a bushy tail that is white underneath and gray above. The North Rim's Kaibab squirrel is dark gray with a bushy all-white tail. Both are ponderosa pine forest residents.

Desert View

esert View offers a panoramic vista of the Painted Desert and Navajo Reservation. The Southwest Indian influence
felt in the Watchtower, which is based on similar structures found in prehistoric Southwest Indian ruins. In the early
00s, architect Mary Jane Colter designed the Watchtower and many other rim buildings to harmonize with the natural
vironment. Nearby, a large, bushy-tailed rock squirrel watches for danger from his lookout boulder.

From Prospecting to Tourism

In the late 1800s, lead, zinc, copper and asbestos were mined in the Grand Canyon. Prospectors improved old India
paths to their claims. These prospectors, like Lewis Boucher (the "hermit" of Hermit's Rest), John Hance, Seth Tanne
William Bass and the Cameron Brothers, were colorful, enterprising characters. Because transporting ore to the rim w:
very difficult, most prospectors turned to "mining tourists" by the 1890s. Many trails bear their names today.

The Bright Angel Trail

mule string, led by an experienced guide, descends the Bright Angel Trail from the South Rim. Both prehistoric and storic Indians used this route to reach their crops at today's Indian Gardens. Miners improved the trail in the late 1800s, d by the early 1900s, it was the main tourist path into the canyon. Today the Bright Angel Trail is part of a major cross- nyon corridor for hikers and mule riders. Many stay overnight at Phantom Ranch on the canyon's floor.

River Runners

River runners enjoy the beauty and challenge of a trip down the Colorado River through the Grand Canyon. The journ
is not as dangerous for these modern adventurers as it was for John Wesley Powell who was exploring unknown territo
but it is still thrilling. Rock walls tower thousands of feet above them, and side canyons promise hidden wonders. Lar
rapids must still be run. At night, the adventurers sleep on beaches under the stars.